Preface

The following book has been developed following our book, *Mindful Empathy: The Mindset of Success for Leaders*. The purpose of this book, along with others written within the *'Mindful Empathy: Interpretations Series* of books, is to invite you to deepen and broaden your mindfulness and empathic interpretive and insight development skills. Simply put, we encourage you, not to just look at these images, but look *into* them, as far as possible remaining focused with single-pointed concentration. We encourage you to look *beyond* what is written.

Deeper meanings and interpretations exist, some explicit, some implicit, some emergent. Mindful Empathic interpretive skill and insight development requires deeper exploration of what cannot be immediately seen. Each page should not be 'read', but *deeply explored*, its texture and deeper meanings allowed to emerge. There is not a right or wrong answer. Commune with the pictures and let them 'speak to you.' Extended mindful exploration of the images and text will not only deepen your interpretive and insightful skill, but also bring a calmness to the act of living within your own reality.

Each pixel, each word has meaning, it is when we spend time mindfully exploring their relationships to each other that we truly experience the depth of mindful reality.

Be kind and enjoy the experience.
Dani & Wayne

Etched Experience

Experiences, not only etched into facial texture, but also into the fabric of our mind.

In the Moment

(Image: Pxhere)

*It is in the moment that our own reality resides. Not in the future,
not in the past, but in the moment.*

Colour

(Image: Pickpik)

Some seek colour in what we see, others seek to be colourful in what others see, it is those who seek both that are most seen.

Embedded Experience

(Image:Pixabay)

Our experiences, while sometimes visible externally, are always embedded internally.

The Eyes Have It

(Image: Needpix)

The Eyes
Servants to the smile.

If the Hat Fits

*Early experience is about trying
on many hats, until one fits in that point in
time. It is where we get those hats,
how we wear those hats, and the best hat for
each purpose that guides us each moment of
our lives.*

Facing Nature

***Our face is reflected in nature
as nature wants our face reflected,
not as we want to be reflected.***

Youthful Joy

(Image: Pikrepo)

The joy of youth, tainted, limited and deeply imbued by experience.

Beauty

(Image: Needpix)

Beauty we expect to extend to the unseen. The stronger the beauty, the stronger our expectation of its existence within the unseen.

Giving & Receiving

Giving: A stronger act than receiving.
Receiving: Dependent on the act of giving.
&
The Process: Reliant on the humble act of receiving with grace.

Realism of Reality

Reality shines a light on the illusion of false belief.

Half of what we see

(Image: Pikrepo)

**Are we guided by the belief of
the half we see, or both halves of what we
think is there?**

What We Say

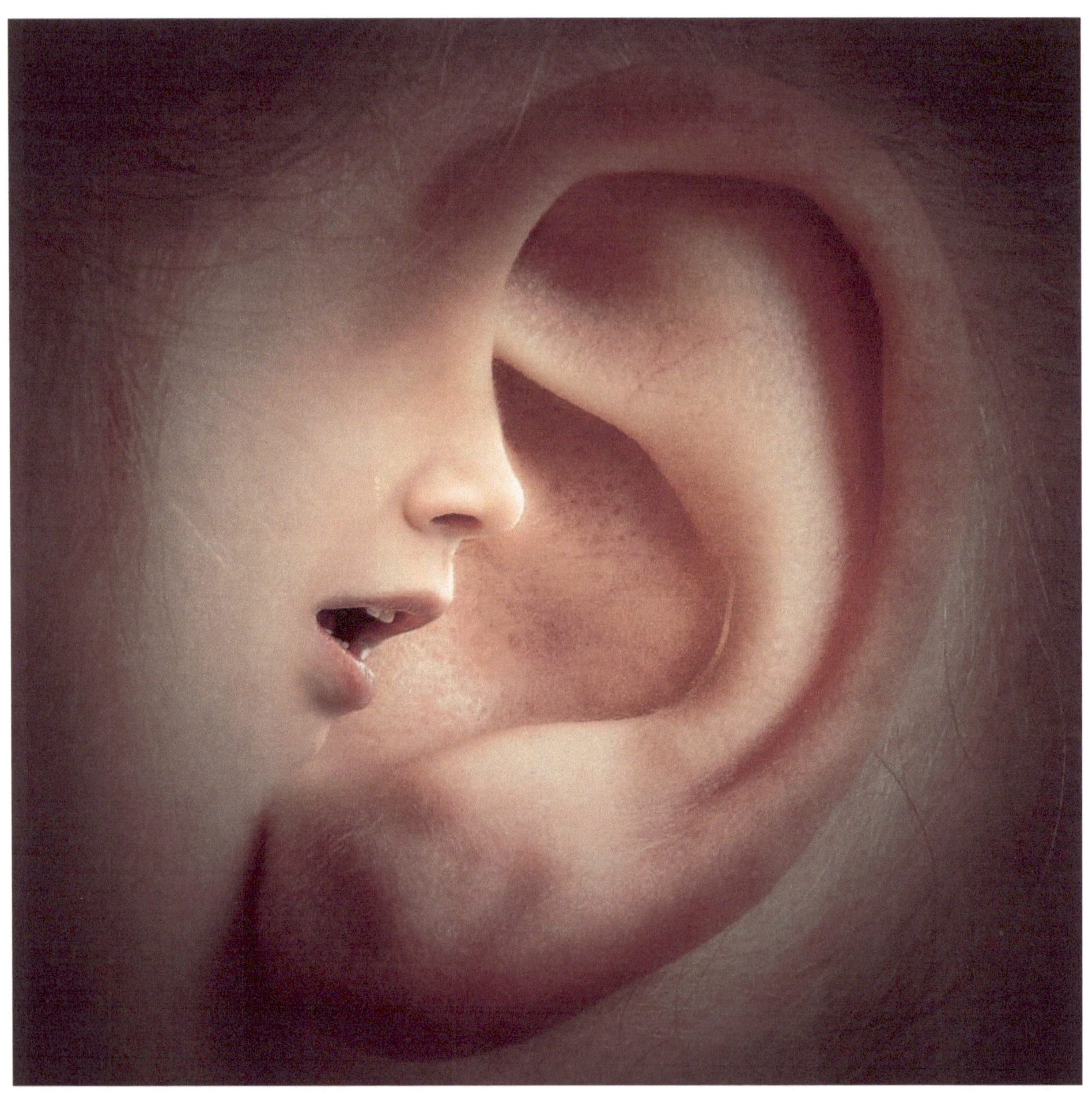

(Image: Pxfuel)

Do we listen to what we say, or do we only hear what others tell us?

Looking with both Eyes

When we are told to look with both eyes, do we need to look only with our own?

Attribution

(Image: Pxfuel)

*The darkness of the world is often attributed
to those we do not truly see.*

Facing the Future

Should we seek to transpose the beauty of humanity to the creations of humanity?

Fear

(Image: Piqsels)

The majority of fear is of humanity's own making.

Our life is a Gift

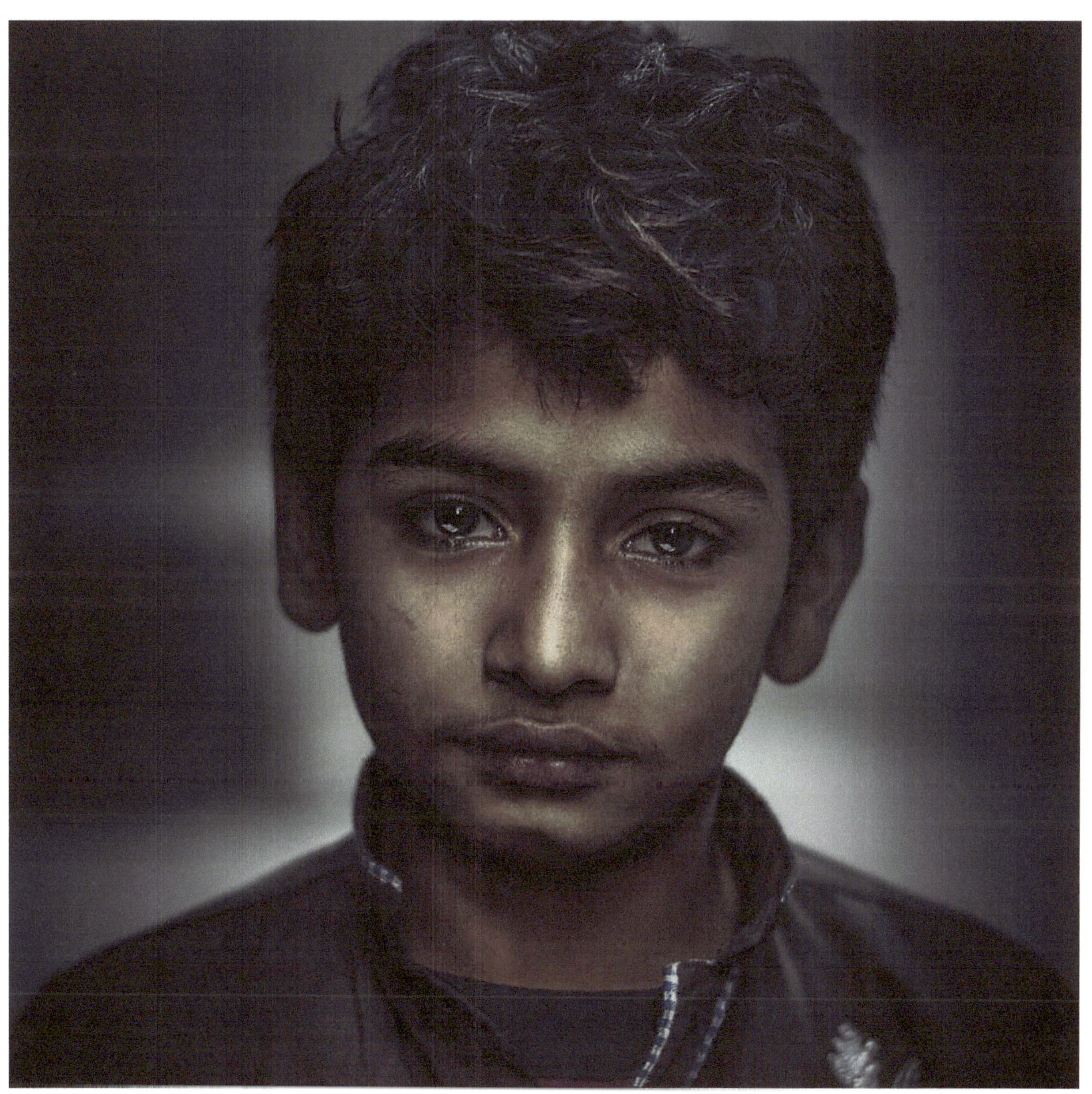

(Image: Pxfuel)

However, the gift of life is not delivered equally.

Hidden Beauty

(Image: Pxfuel)

***The beauty of life, being hidden by
the cloud of progress.***

Wisdom

Wisdom resides in the wise, not the powerful. Although the powerful profess to being wise, the wise rarely profess to being powerful.

Evolution - Devolution

(Image: Pixabay)

From where we evolve, we also return.
Our existence is temporary, our building
blocks returning to eternity.

Only our image Remains

(Image: Pxfuel)

While we may create something memorable, memories fade, only images remain.

Lasting Memories

(Image: Pikrepo)

Thinking of the past can offer absolution, satisfaction, guilt, anger, and sadness to name but a few. The time eventually comes to choose those feelings you wish to leave imprinted in your final memories.